JAPAN 2016 HUMAN RIGHTS REPORT

EXECUTIVE SUMMARY

Japan has a parliamentary government with a constitutional monarchy. Shinzo Abe, leader of the Liberal Democratic Party, became prime minister in 2012. Upper House elections in July were considered free and fair.

Civilian authorities maintained effective control over the security forces.

Leading human rights problems included lack of due process for detention of suspects and poor prison and detention center conditions.

Other persistent human rights problems included detention of asylum seekers; domestic violence, sexual harassment, and workplace discrimination against women; exploitation of children; trafficking in persons, including the exploitation of foreign trainee workers; and societal discrimination against persons with disabilities, minority group members, indigenous persons, and lesbian, gay, bisexual, transgender, and intersex (LGBTI) individuals. There were also concerns over freedom of the press.

The government enforced laws prohibiting human rights abuses and prosecuted officials who committed them.

Section 1. Respect for the Integrity of the Person, Including Freedom from:

a. Arbitrary Deprivation of Life and other Unlawful or Politically Motivated Killings

There were no reports that the government or its agents committed arbitrary or unlawful killings.

b. Disappearance

There were no reports of politically motivated disappearances.

c. Torture and Other Cruel, Inhuman, or Degrading Treatment or Punishment

The law prohibits such practices, and there were no known reports that government officials employed them.

The government continued to deny death row inmates advance information about the date of execution and notified family members of executions after the fact. The government held that this policy spared prisoners the anguish of knowing when they were going to die. Some respected psychologists supported this reasoning; others demurred.

Hazing, bullying, corporal punishment, and sexual harassment continued in the Japanese Self-Defense Forces (JSDF). The Ministry of Defense reported it imposed disciplinary actions for arbitrarily punishing subordinates on 47 JSDF members (out of 247,000 personnel) between April 2014 and March 2015. The Defense Ministry issued guidelines in September 2015 to address bullying and hazing.

Prison and Detention Center Conditions

Prison conditions generally met international standards, although some lacked adequate medical care and sufficient heating in the winter or cooling in the summer.

Physical Conditions: Although the national prison population was significantly less than full capacity at the end of 2014 (most recent data available), the Ministry of Justice reported four of 77 prison facilities were beyond capacity. Authorities held juveniles under age 20 separately from adults in prisons and regular detention centers, but regulations do not require that minors be held separately in immigration detention centers.

In most institutions, extra clothing and blankets provided instead of heating were insufficient to protect inmates against cold weather, according to some local nongovernmental organizations (NGOs). Foreign prisoners in the Tokyo area continued to present chilblains-affected fingers and toes of varying severity resulting from long-term exposure to cold. Press reports noted that following the death of an inmate due to overheating in Osaka in 2015, some detention institutions installed air conditioners and electric fans and provided hand-held fans and rehydrating beverages to help protect inmates against heat.

Some observers documented inadequate medical treatment, including for detainees and prisoners with pre-existing medical conditions. According to the Justice

Ministry, the number of doctors working for correctional institutions was more than 20 percent short of the quota in 2014. Press reported on the deaths of four prisoners during the year. One was a reported suicide, while authorities did not release causes in the other cases. Police and prison authorities were slow in providing treatment for mental illness and have no protocol for offering psychiatric therapy. Foreign observers also noted that dental care was minimal and access to palliative care was lacking. NGOs, lawyers, and doctors continued to criticize medical care in police-operated pre-indictment detention centers, where 10 deaths were reported during the year, and immigration detention centers.

Administration: An NGO reported that in 2015 prison management reduced the use of solitary confinement and set a maximum of three months, with the possibility of extension every month thereafter if deemed necessary.

Authorities regularly hold prisoners condemned to death in solitary confinement until their execution. Authorities allow condemned prisoners visits by family, lawyers, and others. The length of such solitary confinement varies from case to case, and may extend for several years. Prisoners accused of crimes that could lead to the death penalty were also held in solitary confinement before trial, according to an NGO source.

While authorities permitted prisoners and detainees to submit complaints to judicial authorities without censorship and to request investigation of allegations of problematic conditions, they provided the results of such investigations to prisoners in a letter offering little detail beyond a final determination. According to one NGO, in one case the justice minister determined that a decision made by a prison not to allow a prisoner to file a complaint by mail was inappropriate. While there was no prison ombudsman, independent committees (see below, "Monitoring") played the role of an ombudsman.

Independent Monitoring: The government generally allowed visits by NGOs and international organizations.

Prison management regulations stipulate that independent committees inspect prisons and detention centers operated by the Ministry of Justice and detention facilities operated by police. Authorities permitted the committees, which include physicians, lawyers, local municipal officials, and local citizens to interview detainees without the presence of prison officers.

By law third-party inspection committees also inspected immigration detention facilities, and their recommendations generally were given serious consideration.

Domestic and international NGOs and international organizations continued to note that this process failed to meet international prison inspection standards. As examples, they cited the Ministry of Justice's provision of all logistical support for the inspection committees, the use of ministry interpreters during interviews with detainees, and a lack of transparency about the composition of the committees.

The government implemented two laws passed in 2015 establishing inspection committees for governmental training schools and classification homes for juvenile offenders or delinquents below age 20.

d. Arbitrary Arrest or Detention

The law prohibits arbitrary arrest and detention, but credible NGOs and journalists continued to allege that police in large cities employed racial profiling to harass and sometimes arrest "foreign looking" persons, particularly dark-skinned Asians and persons of African descent, without cause.

Role of the Police and Security Apparatus

The National Public Safety Commission, a cabinet-level entity, oversees the National Police Agency (NPA), and prefectural public safety commissions have responsibility for local police forces. The government had effective mechanisms to investigate and punish abuse and corruption. There were no reports of impunity involving the security forces during the year. Some NGOs continued to criticize local public safety commissions for lacking independence from or sufficient authority over police agencies.

Arrest Procedures and Treatment of Detainees

Authorities apprehended persons openly with warrants based on evidence and issued by a duly authorized official and brought detainees before an independent judiciary. Foreign and domestic observers continued to claim that warrants were granted at high rates, detention sometimes occurred notwithstanding weak evidentiary grounds, and multiple repeat arrests of suspects were used to facilitate police case building.

The use of police-operated detention centers placed suspects in the custody of their interrogators. Police sent arrested suspects to police detention facilities in most cases.

The law allows authorities to detain persons for up to 23 days without filing charges.

The law allows detainees, their families, or representatives to request that the court release an indicted detainee on bail. Bail is not available prior to indictment. Reliable NGOs stated that although the practice is illegal, interrogators sometimes offered shortened or suspended sentences to a detainee in exchange for a confession. Provisions of the Penal Procedures Code (revised May 24) that were implemented June 23 enable the court, when it determines whether to allow bail, to take into consideration the extent to which detention would create health, economic, or social disadvantages for detainees; the extent to which it could negatively impact their ability to prepare for trial; and whether a suspect might flee or destroy evidence if released on bail.

Suspects in pretrial detention are legally required to face interrogation. NPA guidelines limit interrogations to a maximum of eight hours and prohibit overnight interrogations. Pre-indictment detainees had access to counsel, including at least one consultation with a court-appointed attorney; counsel, however, may not be present during interrogations.

The law allows police to prohibit detainees from meeting with persons other than counsel if there is probable cause to believe that the suspect may flee or may conceal or destroy evidence (see section 1.d., "Pretrial Detention"). Many detainees, including most charged with drug offenses, were subject to this restriction before indictment, although some were permitted visits from family members in the presence of a detention officer. There is no legal connection between the type of offense and the length of time authorities may deny a detainee visits by family or others. Those detained on drug charges, however, were often denied such visits longer than other suspects, since prosecutors worried that communications with family or others could interfere with investigations.

National Public Safety Commission regulations prohibit police from touching suspects (unless unavoidable), exerting force, threatening them, keeping them in fixed postures for long periods, verbally abusing them, or offering them favors in return for a confession. The NPA announced 28 such cases of abuse in 2015. An NGO asserted that authorities did not adequately enforce the regulations and continued, in some cases, to subject detainees to long interrogation sessions. Media reported on a March 25 Osaka District Court's decision ordering the Osaka Prefectural Police to pay damages to a suspect (who was eventually acquitted) for forcing a confession using coercive techniques during 2013 interrogations.

Prosecutors' offices and police increasingly recorded entire interrogations for heinous criminal cases, cases involving suspects with intellectual or mental disabilities, and other cases on a trial basis. There was no independent oversight. Recording was not mandatory during the year. Local NGOs continued to allege that suspects confessed under duress, mainly during unrecorded interrogations.

Police inspection offices imposed disciplinary actions against some violators of interrogation guidelines, although the NPA did not release related statistics.

<u>Pretrial Detention</u>: Authorities usually held suspects in police-operated detention centers for an initial 72 hours. By law such pre-indictment detention is allowed only where there is probable cause to suspect that a person has committed a crime and is likely to conceal or destroy evidence or flee, but it was used routinely. After interviewing a suspect at the end of the initial 72-hour period, a judge may extend pre-indictment custody for up to two consecutive 10-day periods. Prosecutors routinely sought and received these extensions. Prosecutors may also apply for an additional five-day extension in exceptional cases, such as insurrection, foreign aggression, or violent public assembly.

Because judges customarily grant prosecutorial requests for extensions, pretrial detention, known as daiyou kangoku (substitute prison), usually continued for 23 days. Nearly all persons detained during the year were held in daiyou kangoku. Reliable NGOs and foreign observers continued to report that access to persons other than their attorneys and, in the case of foreign arrestees, consular personnel was denied to persons in daiyou kangoku.

<u>Detainee's Ability to Challenge Lawfulness of Detention before a Court</u>: The law provides detainees the right to a prompt judicial determination of the legality of their detention and requires authorities to inform detainees immediately of the charges against them.

<u>Protracted Detention of Rejected Asylum Seekers or Stateless Persons</u>: Reliable NGOs pointed out that the policy of detaining asylum seekers and other irregular migrants for prolonged periods remained a problem. They noted improvements

from the Ministry of Justice's continuing efforts to streamline the asylum petition process and reduce time spent in detention.

e. Denial of Fair Public Trial

The law provides for an independent judiciary, and the government generally respected judicial independence.

Trial Procedures

The law provides the right to a fair public trial for all citizens. Each charged individual has the right to receive a public trial by an independent civilian court without undue delay (though foreign observers noted that trials may be delayed indefinitely for mentally ill prisoners); has access to defense counsel, including an attorney provided at public expense if indigent; and has the right to cross-examine witnesses. There is a lay judge (jury) system for serious criminal cases, and defendants may not be compelled to testify against themselves. Defendants have the right to be informed promptly and in detail of charges. Authorities provided free interpretation services to foreign defendants in criminal cases. Foreign defendants in civil cases must pay for interpretation, although a judge may order the plaintiff to pay the charges in accordance with a court's final decision.

Defendants are presumed innocent until proven guilty, but credible NGOs and lawyers continued to question whether they were in fact presumed innocent during the legal process. According to NGOs, the majority of indicted detainees confessed while in police custody, although the government continued to assert that convictions were not based primarily on confessions and that interrogation guidelines stipulate that suspects may not be compelled to confess to a crime.

Defendants have the right to appoint their own counsel to prepare a defense, present evidence, and appeal. The court may assist defendants in finding an attorney through a bar association. Defendants may request a court-appointed attorney at state expense if they are unable to afford one.

According to some independent legal scholars, trial procedures favor the prosecution. Observers said a prohibition against defense counsel use of electronic recording devices during interviews with clients undermined counsel effectiveness. The law also does not require full disclosure by prosecutors unless the defending attorney satisfies difficult disclosure procedure conditions, which could lead to the suppression of material favorable to the defense. The May revised procedural code requires, beginning in December, that prosecutors disclose a wider range of evidence in certain cases and provide a list of the evidence they have obtained.

Political Prisoners and Detainees

There were no reports of political prisoners or detainees.

Civil Judicial Procedures and Remedies

There is an independent and impartial judiciary in civil matters. Individuals have access to a court to bring lawsuits seeking damages for, or cessation of, a human rights violation. There are both administrative and judicial remedies for alleged wrongs.

f. Arbitrary or Unlawful Interference with Privacy, Family, Home, or Correspondence

The law prohibits such actions, and the government generally respected these prohibitions.

Section 2. Respect for Civil Liberties, Including:

a. Freedom of Speech and Press

Overall, an independent press, an effective judiciary, and a functioning democratic political system combined to promote freedom of speech and press. The constitution provides for freedom of speech and press, and the government generally respected these freedoms.

During the year, however, several incidents gave rise to concerns about increasing government pressure against critical and independent media. In February, for example, Internal Affairs and Communications Minister Sanae Takaichi reiterated, while denying any plan or intention to take such a step, the government's right to shut down broadcasters that it determined were politically biased. The UN special rapporteur on the right to freedom of opinion and expression said, after a visit in April, "The independence of the press is facing serious threats." He noted "weak legal protection, the … [new] … Specially Designated Secrets Act, and persistent government pressure" as well as the press club system as factors driving his analysis.

<u>Censorship or Content Restrictions</u>: Media expressed a wide variety of views without overt restriction. Nonetheless, members of the press, including major newspapers and broadcasters, privately voiced concerns that the government indirectly encouraged self-censorship practices within major media outlets. A Reporters Without Borders survey concluded that media self-censorship has risen in response to legal changes and government criticism. Some journalists, media analysts, and NGOs continued to criticize press (kisha) clubs as encouraging self-censorship and co-opting journalists. These clubs are formed in individual organizations, including ministries, and may block nonmembers from covering the organization.

Internet Freedom

The government did not restrict or disrupt access to the internet or censor online content, and there were no credible reports that the government monitored private online communications without appropriate legal authority. The internet was widely accessible and used.

Academic Freedom and Cultural Events

The Ministry of Education's approval process for history textbooks, particularly its treatment of the country's 20th century colonial and military history, was a subject of controversy.

The national anthem and flag continued to attract some controversy. Press reports noted occasional cases of disciplinary action against public school teachers for refusing to stand and sing the national anthem in front of the flag.

b. Freedom of Peaceful Assembly and Association

The law provides for freedom of assembly and association, and the government generally respected these rights.

c. Freedom of Religion

See the Department of State's *International Religious Freedom Report* at www.state.gov/religiousfreedomreport/.

d. Freedom of Movement, Internally Displaced Persons, Protection of Refugees, and Stateless Persons

The law provides for freedom of internal movement, foreign travel, emigration, and repatriation, and the government generally respected these rights. The government cooperated with the Office of the UN High Commissioner for Refugees and other humanitarian organizations in providing protection and assistance to internally displaced persons, refugees, asylum seekers, stateless persons, and other persons of concern.

Internally Displaced Persons

The government generally provided adequate shelter and other protective services in the aftermath of the 2011 earthquake, tsunami, and nuclear power plant disaster in Fukushima Prefecture and sought to provide permanent relocation or reconstruction options. According to Reconstruction Agency statistics, as of December 9, approximately 130,000 evacuees remained displaced, far fewer than in 2015.

Protection of Refugees

Access to Asylum: The law provides for granting asylum or refugee status, and the government has established a system for providing protection to refugees who were already resident in the country. The government, however, granted refugee status exceedingly rarely.

There were 7,586 applicants for refugee status in 2015, the largest number since the country began recognizing refugee status and more than a 50-percent increase compared with 2014. Authorities granted refugee status to 27 individuals.

Refugee and asylum applicants may ask lawyers to participate in their hearings before refugee examiners. Although government-funded legal support was not available for most refugee and asylum seekers requesting it, the Federation of Bar Associations continued to fund a program that provided free legal assistance to those applicants who lacked financial means.

Members of the government, the Federation of Bar Associations, and the NGO Forum for Refugees Japan extended a pilot project to provide accommodation, casework, and legal services for individuals who arrived at Narita airport, received temporary landing or provisional stay permission, and sought refugee status.

<u>Refoulement</u>: The government does not expel or return refugees to countries where their lives or freedom would be threatened, in accordance with the UN Convention and Protocol relating to the Status of Refugees. Responding to criticism of the government's high threshold for proof in the adjudication of asylum applications, in September 2015 the Ministry of Justice announced new operational guidelines for refugee and asylum adjudication that stipulate that foreigners fleeing conflict in their country of origin may be granted "shelter from conflict," if not refugee status. Some activists continue to criticize the government's criteria as outside of the international norm.

There were no reported cases of refoulement of asylum seekers during the year.

<u>Employment</u>: Applicants for refugee status normally may not work unless they have valid short-term visas. They must apply for permission to engage in income-earning activities before the visas expire. In the interim before approval, the Refugee Assistance Headquarters, a section of the government-funded, public interest, incorporated Foundation for the Welfare and Education of the Asian People, provided small stipends to some applicants who faced financial difficulties.

<u>Access to Basic Services</u>: Refugees continued to face the same discrimination patterns as other foreigners: reduced access to housing, education, and employment. Except for those who met right-to-work conditions, individuals whose refugee applications were pending or on appeal did not have the right to receive social welfare. This status rendered them completely dependent on overcrowded government shelters, illegal employment, or NGO assistance.

<u>Temporary Protection</u>: In 2015 the government provided temporary protection to 79 individuals who may not qualify as refugees, 31 fewer than in 2014.

Section 3. Freedom to Participate in the Political Process

The law provides citizens the ability to choose their government through free and fair periodic elections held by secret ballot and based on universal and equal suffrage, and citizens exercised that ability.

Elections and Political Participation

<u>Recent Elections</u>: In July--for the third time on the sitting government's watch--the country held a nationwide vote for the Upper House of the National Diet (parliament), which was generally regarded as free and fair.

<u>Participation of Women and Minorities</u>: The constitution stipulates women's right to participate in political processes, and authorities protected these rights. Women held 44 of 475 seats in parliament's Lower House and 50 of 242 seats in the Upper House after the July Upper House election. Women held three of the 19 seats in the cabinet following the August 3 cabinet shuffle and none of the three senior posts in the ruling Liberal Democratic Party. At the end of 2016, there were three female governors out of 47 prefectures. The reasons for the limited female participation in political life are complex and under close scrutiny by the government and academia. During the year, Yuriko Koike was elected Tokyo's first female governor and Renho Murata was elected as the first female leader (and the first person with mixed ethnic heritage) of a major political party (the Democratic Party).

Because some ethnic minority group members are of mixed heritage and did not self-identify, it was difficult to determine their numbers in the Diet. At least two Diet members were naturalized Japanese citizens, including Renho.

Section 4. Corruption and Lack of Transparency in Government

The law provides criminal penalties for corruption by officials, and the government generally implemented the law effectively. Officials sometimes engaged in corrupt practices. Independent academic experts stated that ties among politicians, bureaucrats, and businesspersons were close and corruption remained a concern. NGOs continued to criticize the practice of retired senior public servants taking high-paying jobs with private firms that rely on government contracts. The Ministry of Justice reported prosecutions of 85 suspects for bribery in 2015, and the Supreme Court reported convictions of 41 individuals for bribery in 2015. There were regular media reports of investigations into financial and accounting irregularities involving high-profile politicians and government officials. Minister of Economy, Trade, and Industry Akira Amari resigned from his cabinet-level post on January 28 while retaining his seat in the Diet. He ultimately resumed full parliamentary activities on August 1 after local prosecutors decided not to indict him on influence-peddling charges. There were cases of improper use of public funds for political activities by prefectural and municipal assembly members, with the resignation of 12 of 40 members of the Toyama City Assembly a notable example.

<u>Corruption</u>: Several government agencies are involved in combating corruption, including the NPA and the National Tax Administration Agency. In addition, the

Fair Trade Commission enforces anti-monopoly law to prevent unreasonable restraint of trade and unfair business practices, such as bid rigging. The Japan Financial Intelligence Center is responsible for preventing money laundering and terrorist financing. The National Public Services Ethics Board polices public servants suspected of ethics violations. The Board of Audit monitors the accounts of corporations in which the government is a majority shareholder. Anticorruption agencies generally operated independently, effectively, and with adequate resources, although some experienced staffing shortfalls.

Financial Disclosure: The law requires members of the Diet to disclose publicly their income and assets (except for ordinary savings), including ownership of real estate, securities, and transportation means. The law requires governors, prefectural assembly members, mayors, and assembly members of twenty major cities to disclose their incomes and assets based on their local ordinances but does not require assembly members of the remaining approximately 1,720 municipalities to do the same. There are no penalties for false disclosure. The law does not apply to nonelected officials. NGOs and media criticized the law as lax. Separately, the cabinet-approved code provides that cabinet ministers, senior vice-ministers, and parliamentary vice-ministers publicly disclose their, their spouses', and their dependent children's assets.

Public Access to Information: By law the public has the right to access government information, although observers sometimes claimed the government did not willingly disclose information. Local municipality employees sometimes disclosed the identities of those seeking information pertaining to allegations of improper use of public funds by local politicians to the politicians themselves. The Ministry of Internal Affairs and Communications subsequently requested on September 30 that all governors and municipal assemblies' chairs take steps to protect the identities of those seeking such information, so as not to discourage information disclosure requests or undermine the reliability of the information disclosure system.

Section 5. Governmental Attitude Regarding International and Nongovernmental Investigation of Alleged Violations of Human Rights

A number of domestic and international human rights groups generally operated without government restriction, investigating and publishing their findings on human rights cases. Government officials usually were cooperative and responsive to their views.

<u>Government Human Rights Bodies</u>: The Justice Ministry's Human Rights Counseling Office has 315 offices across the nation. Approximately 14,000 volunteers fielded questions in person, by telephone, or on the internet and provided confidential consultations. Counselling in a foreign language was available in several offices. Some claimed these offices only field queries and do not have authority to investigate human rights violations by individuals or public organizations, provide counsel, or mediate. Municipal governments have human rights offices that dealt with a range of human rights problems.

There was no independent ombudsman office at the national level, although the Administrative Counseling System, a department of the Ministry of Internal Affairs and Communications, was well resourced and provided many of the same functions as an ombudsman's office. Its director general represented the country on international ombudsman bodies.

Section 6. Discrimination, Societal Abuses, and Trafficking in Persons

Women

<u>Rape and Domestic Violence</u>: The law criminalizes all forms of rape involving force against women. The law does not deny spousal rape, but no court has ever ruled on such a case, except in situations of marital breakdown (i.e., formal or informal separation, etc.). The law defines rape as "forcible sexual intercourse through assault or intimidation with a female of not less than 13 years of age or sexual intercourse with a female under 13 years of age." The law mandates a minimum of three years in prison with work for a defined term. Courts have interpreted "forcible" to mean that physical resistance by the victim is necessary to find that a sexual encounter was rape. Observers pointed out a lack of training for judges, prosecutors, and lawyers to understand sexual crimes and victims.

A 2015 Cabinet Office survey showed that only 4.3 percent of women who suffered forcible sexual intercourse reported the crime to police. Observers attributed women's reluctance to report rape to a variety of factors, including a lack of victim support, potential secondary victimization through the police response, and court proceedings that lack understanding for rape victims.

Although prohibited by law, domestic violence against women remained a serious problem, according to multiple sources. Victims of abuse by domestic partners, spouses, and former spouses could receive protection at shelters and seek restraining orders from court.

NGOs reported a number of cases in which companies deceived women, and in some cases men, with "modeling" contracts that required performance in pornographic videos. The companies demanded breach of contract payments when the women and men refused to act in the videos. In two cases, police arrested representatives of major show business agencies for dispatching women to act in pornographic videos. In one case, a court fined an agency president and staffers in June. Police announced in October that they had sent the other case to prosecutors.

Japan began implementing the 2015 agreement with the Republic of Korea on World War II "comfort women" (women trafficked for sexual purposes). While the agreement remains controversial with some civil society groups, the government provided the agreed one billion yen ($9.7 million) contribution to a foundation established by the Republic of Korea to provide support for the former "comfort women."

Sexual Harassment: The law does not criminalize sexual harassment but includes measures to identify companies that fail to prevent it, and prefectural labor offices and the Ministry of Health, Labor, and Welfare provided these companies with advice, guidance, and recommendations. Companies that fail to comply with government guidance may be publicly identified, and although this is extremely rare, it has begun to happen. Sexual harassment in the workplace remained widespread (see section 7.d.).

A stalker control law prohibits e-mail harassment.

Reproductive Rights: Couples and individuals have the right to decide freely and responsibly the number, spacing, and timing of their children; manage their reproductive health; and have the information and means to do so, free from discrimination, coercion, and violence. Women had access to contraception and maternal health services, including skilled attendance during childbirth, prenatal care, and essential obstetric and postpartum care.

Discrimination: The law prohibits gender discrimination and generally provides women the same rights as men. The Gender Equality Bureau in the Cabinet Office continued to examine policies and monitor developments.

Despite these policies, NGOs continued to allege that implementation of antidiscrimination measures was insufficient, pointing to discriminatory provisions in the law, unequal treatment of women in the labor market (see section 7.d.), and low representation of women in high-level elected bodies. NGOs urged the government to abolish a six-month waiting period stipulated in the law for women, but not men, before remarriage; eliminate different age minimums for marriage depending on sex; and allow married couples a choice of surnames. In late 2015 the Supreme Court upheld the practice of one surname per household, but ruled that the six-month waiting period for women before remarriage was unconstitutional and recommended the ban be shortened to 100 days. On June 1, the Diet passed a Civil Code revision, which took effect on June 7, to shorten the ban on remarriage to 100 days and allow remarriage even earlier if a doctor's examination showed the woman was not pregnant.

Children

Birth Registration: The law grants citizenship at birth to a child of the following: a Japanese father who either is married to the child's mother or recognizes his paternity, a Japanese mother, or a child born in the country to parents who are both unknown or are stateless. The law requires registration within 14 days after in-country birth or within three months after birth abroad, and these deadlines were generally met. Individuals were allowed to register births after the deadline but were required to pay a fine.

The law requires birth entries in the family registry to specify whether a child was born in or out of wedlock, but the law no longer denies full inheritance rights to children born out of wedlock. The law presumes that a child born within 300 days of a divorce is the divorced man's child, resulting in the nonregistration of an unknown number of children.

Child Abuse: Reports of child abuse increased due to increased public awareness, according to the Ministry of Health, Labor, and Welfare. During the period from April 2015 through March 2016, local child guidance centers acted on a record-high 103,260 reports of child abuse by parents or guardians. According to the NPA, 822 child abuse cases from January to December 2015, including parent-child suicides, parental abandonment, and abuse by parents or guardians, led to 849 arrests and the death of 58 children. A law against bullying went into full effect during the year, but school bullying was on the rise, recording 224,540 cases at public elementary, junior high, and high schools from April 2015 through March 2016, as the Ministry of Education, Culture, Sports, Science, and Technology reported. Sexual abuse of female and male children by teachers was reported.

The government revised the law on May 27 to simplify the process of inspecting homes where child abuse is suspected; require child welfare offices to have legal, psychological, and medical experts; allow more municipalities to have child welfare offices; and raise the age of eligibility for staying at public homes.

Early and Forced Marriage: The law stipulates that to marry, the male partner must be age 18 or older and the female partner, 16 or older. A person under 20 may not marry without at least one parent's approval.

Sexual Exploitation of Children: Child prostitution is illegal, with a penalty of imprisonment with labor for up to five years or a fine of up to three million yen ($27,600) for adult offenders and penalties of up to seven years' imprisonment and fines of up to 10 million yen ($92,000) for traffickers. The continued practice of enjo kosai (compensated dating) and the existence of websites for online dating, social networking, and "delivery health" (a euphemism for call-girl or escort services) facilitated the sex trafficking of children and other commercial sex industries. A trend known as "JK business" continued to grow; these businesses include cafes that feature underage female servers and massage parlors staffed by high school-age girls. NGOs helping girls in "JK business" reported a link between these activities and the exploitation of children in prostitution.

Statutory rape laws criminalize sexual intercourse with a girl younger than 13, notwithstanding her consent. The penalty for statutory rape is not less than three years' imprisonment with mandatory labor, and the law was enforced. Additionally, national law and local ordinances comprehensively address sexual abuse of minors, including boy victims.

The country was a site for the production of child pornography and the exploitation of children by traffickers. By law since 2014, the possession of child pornography is a crime; enforcement began in July 2015. The commercialization of child pornography is illegal; the penalty is imprisonment with labor for not more than three years or a fine not exceeding three million yen ($27,600), and police continued to crack down on this crime. Police reported a record-high 1,938 child pornography investigations involving 905 child victims in 2015.

No law addresses the unfettered availability of sexually explicit cartoons, comics, and video games, some of which depicted scenes of violent sexual abuse and the rape of children. Experts suggested a culture that appears to accept the depiction of child sexual abuse harmed children.

See the Department of State's *Trafficking in Persons Report* at
www.state.gov/j/tip/rls/tiprpt/.

International Child Abductions: The country is a party to the 1980 Hague
Convention on the Civil Aspects of International Child Abduction. See the
Department of State's *Annual Report on International Parental Child Abduction* at
travel.state.gov/content/childabduction/en/legal/compliance.html.

Anti-Semitism

The Jewish population was approximately 2,000. There were no reports of anti-
Semitic acts in 2016.

Trafficking in Persons

See the Department of State's *Trafficking in Persons Report* at
www.state.gov/j/tip/rls/tiprpt/.

Persons with Disabilities

The Basic Act for Persons with Disabilities prohibits discrimination against
persons with physical, intellectual, mental and other disabilities affecting body and
mind and bars infringement of their rights and interests on the grounds of disability
in public and private sector. The Act on the Elimination of Discrimination against
Persons with Disabilities effective in April requires the public sector to provide
reasonable accommodations and the private sector to make best efforts in
employment, education, access to health care, or the provision of other services.
The laws do not stipulate remedies for persons with disabilities who suffer
discriminatory acts or penalties for noncompliance.

The law requires the public sector to provide reasonable accommodation and
stipulates that the private sector shall "make efforts" to do so. Advocacy groups
for individuals with disabilities were broadly supportive of the legislation.
Nonetheless, persons with disabilities faced limited access to some public sector
services.

The law mandates that the government and private companies hire minimum
proportions (2 percent) of persons with disabilities (including mental disabilities)
or be fined. Disability rights advocates claimed that some companies preferred to
pay the fine rather than hire persons with disabilities (see section 7.d.).

Accessibility laws mandate that new construction projects for public use must include provisions for persons with disabilities. The government may grant low interest loans and tax benefits to operators of hospitals, theaters, hotels, and other public facilities if they upgrade or install features to accommodate persons with disabilities.

While some schools provided inclusive education, children with disabilities generally attended specialized schools.

Mental health professionals criticized as insufficient the government's efforts to reduce the stigma of mental illness and inform the public that depression and other mental illnesses are treatable and biologically based. Abuse of persons with disabilities was a serious concern. Persons with disabilities around the country suffered abuse by family members, care facility employees, or employers. Private surveys indicated discrimination against, and sexual abuse of, women with disabilities.

A former employee of a center for persons with disabilities in the city of Sagamihara has been charged with the July stabbing to death of 19, and injury of 26, patients at the center, the largest number of people to die in a mass killing in the country in decades. Local police subsequently declined to release the identities of the victims, citing privacy concerns for their families. Some disabilities advocates criticized this nondisclosure of names as tacitly endorsing the views of those who say persons with disabilities should be kept separate from the rest of society. The suspect had previously posted threats on social media, including "It would be better for severely disabled to die" and his plan "to visit many facilities and kill 600 by October [starting] with the facility where I was."

National/Racial/Ethnic Minorities

Minorities experienced varying degrees of societal discrimination.

The Diet passed in December the Act on the Elimination of Discrimination against Buraku (the descendants of feudal-era outcasts), the first law solely addressing discrimination against Buraku. According to the Act, effective as of December, the national and local governments will study discrimination against Buraku, implement awareness education, and enhance the counseling system. Buraku advocacy groups continued to report that despite socioeconomic improvements achieved by many Buraku, widespread discrimination persisted in employment, marriage, housing, and property assessment. While the Buraku label was no longer officially used to identify individuals, the family registry system could be used to identify them and facilitate discriminatory practices. Buraku advocates expressed concern that employers who require family registry information from job applicants for background checks, including many government agencies, may use this information to identify and discriminate against Buraku applicants.

Despite legal safeguards against discrimination, foreign nationals with permanent residency in the country, including many who were born, raised, and educated in the country, were subjected to various forms of entrenched societal discrimination, including restricted access to housing, education, health care, and employment opportunities. Foreign nationals as well as "foreign looking" Japanese citizens reported they were prohibited entry, sometimes by signs reading "Japanese Only," to privately owned facilities serving the public, including hotels and restaurants. Although such discrimination was usually open and direct, NGOs complained of government failure to enforce laws prohibiting such restrictions.

Societal acceptance of ethnic Koreans who were permanent residents or citizens generally continued to improve. Although authorities approved most naturalization applications, advocacy groups continued to complain about excessive bureaucratic hurdles that complicated the naturalization process and a lack of transparent criteria for approval. Ethnic Koreans who chose not to naturalize faced difficulties in terms of civil and political rights and, according to the country's periodic submissions to the UN Committee on the Elimination of Racial Discrimination, regularly encountered discrimination in access to housing, education, and other benefits.

Ultra-right-wing groups used racially pejorative terms and were accused of hate speech by press and politicians. Senior government officials publicly repudiated the harassment of ethnic groups as inciting discrimination and reaffirmed the protection of individual rights for everyone in the country.

Following passage of a law on hate speech in May, Osaka City passed the first local ordinance to counter hate speech in July. On September 27, the Osaka District Court found the former chairman of the extremist, ultra-nationalist political organization "Zaitokukai," Makoto Sakurai, personally liable for emotional pain suffered by Lee Shin-Hye, a freelance journalist, due to hate speech, and ordered Zaitokukai to pay 770,000 yen ($7,084) in damages. According to the ruling, derogatory statements were delivered both online and through public loudspeaker messaging. Judge Tamami Masumori said that Sakurai and Zaitokukai maliciously insulted Lee beyond a socially tolerable level and slandered Lee's journalistic work.

According to media and NGO reports, incidents of hate speech on the internet continued.

Although the Supreme Court has ruled that foreign permanent residents are not entitled to welfare because they are not Japanese citizens, municipalities customarily provided needy foreign permanent residents with stipends. Following the court decision, moreover, the minister of health, labor, and welfare reaffirmed that the government would continue to provide benefits to foreign residents for humanitarian reasons.

A Pension Agency enforcement directive allows employers to forgo pension and insurance contributions on behalf of their foreign employees who teach languages, as opposed to Japanese employees in similar positions. Employers may use different contracts for foreigners than for nationals, and courts generally upheld this distinction as nondiscriminatory.

Indigenous People

Although the Ainu enjoy the same rights as all other citizens, when clearly identifiable as Ainu, they faced discrimination. The law emphasizes preservation of Ainu culture but lacks some provisions that Ainu groups have demanded, such as recognition for land claims, reserved seats in the Diet and local assemblies, and a government apology for previous policies. The government recognizes the Ainu as an indigenous people in parliamentary proceedings, although the recognition had no legal ramifications.

On March 25, Hokkaido University and the Ainu reached an out-of-court settlement in a long-running case about the return of Ainu remains. The university returned the bones of 11 persons to the town of Kineusu in July. The original plaintiffs and other Ainu people welcomed the remains back to the cemetery with a series of traditional Ainu funeral ceremonies. The lawsuit was the first in the country in which indigenous persons asserted indigenous group (rather than individual) rights.

In the 2015 election, a Sapporo City assemblyman, who had claimed that there were "no more Ainu people" and criticized government policies for privileging self-identified Ainu, lost his seat. The income of self-identified Ainu continued to be less than surrounding Japanese.

To address concerns about treatment of Ainu remains used in academic research, in 2015 the government announced it would build a memorial facility where the unidentifiable remains of Ainu would be interred. The Ainu Association welcomed the government plan, but continued to request assistance in identifying and returning remains to descendants or to hometowns.

Although the government does not recognize the Ryukyu (a term that includes residents of Okinawa and portions of Kagoshima Prefecture) as indigenous people, it officially acknowledged their unique culture and history and made efforts to preserve and show respect for those traditions.

Acts of Violence, Discrimination, and Other Abuses Based on Sexual Orientation and Gender Identity

No law prohibits discrimination based on sexual orientation or gender identity. In general, societal acceptance of LGBTI persons continued to improve. There are no existing penalties associated with such discrimination, and no related statistics were available. Laws governing rape, sexual commerce, and other activity involving sexual intercourse do not apply to same-sex sexual activity, since the law defines sex as exclusively male-to-female vaginal intercourse. This definition leads to lower penalties for perpetrators of male rape and greater legal ambiguity surrounding same-sex prostitution.

NGOs that advocate on behalf of LGBTI persons reported no impediments to organization but some instances of bullying, harassment, and violence. Stigma surrounding LGBTI persons remained an impediment to self-reporting of discrimination or abuse, and studies on bullying and violence in schools generally did not take into account the sexual orientation or gender identity of the persons involved. Pervasive societal stigma surrounding LGBTI persons also prevented many from being open about their sexual orientation, and attorneys who frequently represent LGBTI persons related several cases during the year in which clients were threatened with disclosure of sexual orientation. Self-censorship in the press remained an impediment to bringing LGBTI issues into mainstream discourse.

The law allows transgender individuals to change their legal gender, but only after receiving a diagnosis of sexual identity disorder.

HIV and AIDS Social Stigma

No law prohibits discrimination against persons with HIV/AIDS, although nonbinding Ministry of Health, Labor, and Welfare guidelines state that firms should not terminate or fail to hire individuals based on their HIV status. Courts have awarded damages to individuals fired from positions due to that status.

Concern about discrimination against individuals with HIV/AIDS and the stigma associated with the disease prevented many persons from disclosing their HIV/AIDS status. According to NGOs, fear of dismissal caused many individuals to hide their HIV/AIDS status.

Section 7. Worker Rights

a. Freedom of Association and the Right to Collective Bargaining

The law provides for the right of private sector workers to form and join unions of their choice without previous authorization or excessive requirements and protects their rights to strike and bargain collectively.

The law places limitations on the right of public sector workers and employees of state-owned enterprises to form and join unions of their choice. Public sector employees do not have the right to strike; trade union leaders who incite a strike in the public sector may be dismissed and fined or imprisoned for up to three years. Public sector employees may participate in public service employee unions, which may negotiate collectively with their employers on wages, hours, and other conditions of employment. Firefighting personnel and prison officers are prohibited from organizing collectively and do not possess the right to conclude a collective bargaining agreement.

Workers in sectors providing essential services, including electric power generation and transmission, transportation and railways, telecommunications, medical care and public health, and the postal service must give 10 days' advance notice to authorities before organizing a strike. Employees involved in providing essential services do not have the right to collective bargaining. The law prohibits antiunion discrimination and provides for the reinstatement of workers fired for union activities.

The government effectively enforced laws providing for freedom of association and collective bargaining. In the case of a violation, a worker or union may lodge an objection with the Labor Committee, which may issue a relief order for action by the employer. A plaintiff may then take the matter to a civil court. If the court upholds the relief order and determines that a violation of that order has occurred, it may impose a fine of less than one million yen ($9,200) and/or imprisonment of less than one year. Government oversight and these penalties were generally sufficient to deter violations.

The government and employers respected freedom of association and the right to collective bargaining, but increasing use of short-term contracts undermined regular employment and frustrated organizing efforts. Collective bargaining was common in the private sector, although some businesses changed their form of incorporation to a holding company structure, not legally considered employers, to circumvent employee protections under the law.

b. Prohibition of Forced or Compulsory Labor

The law prohibits all forms of forced or compulsory labor.

The government effectively enforced the law, although there were small segments of the labor market, such as some categories of foreign workers, where violations persisted and enforcement could be strengthened. Legal penalties for forced labor varied depending on its form, the victim(s), and the law that prosecutors used to prosecute such offenses. Not all forms of forced or compulsory labor were subject to sufficient penalties. For example, for recruitment for forced labor, the law allows maximum punishment of a fine of 200,000 yen ($1,840), which was not sufficient to deter violations. Some NGOs argued that the legal definition for forced labor cases was too narrow.

Authorities applied labor laws to punish legal violations detected in the Technical Intern Training Program (TITP). This program allows foreign workers to enter the country and work for up to three years in a de facto guest worker program. Inspectors from the Ministry of Health, Labor, and Welfare and local immigration inspectors under the Ministry of Justice inspected TITP workplaces that employed interns under the program. NGOs maintained that oversight was insufficient. The prescribed governmental response to noncompliance in the TITP program, for instance, was to issue warnings and advisories and ban companies from future participation in the TITP for a period of one to five years. The Health, Labor, and Welfare Ministry does not have legal authority to inspect Japanese recruiting organizations. Of the more than 30,000 workplaces employing TITP workers in 2015, the ministry investigated 5,173 workplaces of concern and found violations of working hours, safety standards, payment of overtime wages, and other regulations at 3,695 of them. The ministry instructed the TITP employers to take corrective actions, and in 46 cases where they failed to act, the ministry referred the cases to public prosecutors.

Reports of forced labor continued in the manufacturing, construction, and shipbuilding sectors, largely in small- and medium-size enterprises employing foreign nationals through the TITP. Workers in these jobs experienced restrictions on freedom of movement and communication with persons outside the program, nonpayment of wages, high debts to brokers in countries of origin, and retention of identity documents. Workers were also sometimes subjected to "forced savings" that they forfeited by leaving early or being forcibly repatriated. For example, some technical interns reportedly paid up to one million yen ($9,200) in their home countries for jobs and were reportedly employed under contracts that mandate forfeiture in their home countries of the equivalent of thousands of dollars if workers try to leave, both of which are illegal under the TITP. Workers who entered the country illegally or who overstayed their visas were particularly vulnerable.

On November 18, the Diet approved a revision to the TITP law that establishes a new Supervisory Body to oversee entities receiving technical interns and establishes new penalties in case of violations. The revision also extends the maximum term of participation in the TITP from 3 years to 5 years, which is expected to expand the use of the program.

Also see the Department of State's *Trafficking in Persons Report* at www.state.gov/j/tip/rls/tiprpt/.

c. Prohibition of Child Labor and Minimum Age for Employment

Children between ages 15 and 18 may perform any job that is not designated as dangerous or harmful, such as handling heavy objects or cleaning, inspecting, or repairing machinery while it is in operation. Children between ages 15 and 18 are prohibited from working late night shifts. Children between 13 and 15 may perform "light labor" only, and children under 13 may work only in the entertainment industry.

The government effectively enforced these laws. Penalties for child labor violations included fines and imprisonment and were sufficient to deter violations.

Children were subjected to commercial sexual exploitation (see section 6, "Children").

d. Discrimination with Respect to Employment and Occupation

The law prohibits discrimination with respect to employment and occupation based on race, sex, personal or political beliefs, national origin or citizenship, social status or origin, disability, age, and some communicable diseases, such as leprosy. The law does not explicitly prohibit discrimination with respect to employment and occupation based on sexual orientation and/or gender identity, HIV-positive status, or language. Labor law does not explicitly prohibit discrimination based on religion. The law also mandates equal pay for men and women. The law mandates that the government and private companies hire minimum proportions (2 percent) of persons with disabilities (including mental disabilities). By law companies with more than 200 employees that do not comply with requirements to hire minimum proportions of persons with disabilities must pay a fine of 50,000 yen ($460) per vacant position per month.

Enforcement regulations of the equal employment opportunity law also include prohibitions against policies or practices that were not adopted with discriminatory intent but which have a discriminatory effect (called "indirect discrimination" in law) for all workers in recruitment, hiring, promotion, and changes of job type. Enforcement of these provisions was generally weak.

On March 29, the Diet passed revisions to the Child-care and Nursing-care Leave Law and the Equal Employment Opportunity Law. The revisions take effect January 1, 2017. The revised leave law is expected to offer greater flexibility in taking family care leave, for example, by allowing employees to divide their permitted leave into three separate instances. It also is designed to ease the eligibility of fixed-term contract workers to take child-care leave. The revised employment law would obligate employers to take measures to prevent maternity harassment. On April 1, a 2015 law took effect that required national and local governments, as well as private sector companies that employ at least 301 people, to analyze women's employment in their organizations and release action plans to promote women's participation and advancement. Shortly thereafter, the Ministry of Health, Labor, and Welfare made public data reported by individual firms on the state of women's employment.

In cases of violations, the Ministry of Health, Labor, and Welfare may request the employers to report the matter, and the ministry may issue advice, instructions, or corrective guidance. If the employer does not follow the ministry's guidance, the employer's name may be disclosed. If the employer fails to report or files a false report, the employer may be subject to a fine of less than 200,000 yen ($1,840).

Government hotlines in prefectural labor bureau equal employment departments handled consultations concerning sexual harassment and mediated disputes when possible.

Women continued to express concern about unequal treatment in the workforce. Women's average monthly wage was approximately 70 percent of that of men. Sexual harassment in the workplace remained widespread. In the first survey of its kind, the ministry reported that 30 percent of women in full- and part-time employment reported being sexually harassed at work. Among full-time workers, the figure was 35 percent.

There also continued to be cases of employers forcing pregnant women to leave their jobs. The ministry reported that the number of cases in which people sought advice from labor authorities regarding maternity harassment during fiscal year 2015, the latest year for which such data were available, increased 19 percent from the previous year. In 2015 the ministry announced the name of an employer who had unfairly dismissed a female employee due to pregnancy and repeatedly refused to follow the ministry's corrective guidance. The ministry stated this was the first time it disclosed the name of an employer pursuant to the law. In a separate 2015 case, the Hiroshima High Court ordered a local hospital to pay 1.75 million yen ($16,100) in damages to a physical therapist who was demoted after seeking a lighter workload due to pregnancy.

The government increased child-care facilities, along with encouraging private companies to report gender statistics in annual financial reports. In 2014, the latest year for which such data were available, statistics from the ministry showed that while persons with disabilities comprised approximately 2.2 to 2.3 percent of public sector employees, the private sector did not reach minimum proportions required by law; persons with disabilities comprised approximately 1.8 percent of employees. Disability rights advocates claimed that some companies preferred to pay a fine rather than hire persons with disabilities.

In August the Japanese Trade Union Confederation released a survey that noted 23 percent of respondents reported that they had personally experienced or observed LGBTI-related harassment at their place of employment or at work-related activities.

e. Acceptable Conditions of Work

Beginning in October, the revised minimum wage ranged from 714 yen ($6.57) to 932 yen ($8.57) per hour (depending on the prefecture), up by an average of 25 yen ($0.05) compared with 2015. The poverty line was 1.22 million yen ($11,225) per year.

The law provides for a 40-hour workweek for most industries and, with exceptions, limits the number of overtime hours permitted in a fixed period. It mandates premium pay of no less than 25 percent for more than eight hours of work in a day, up to 45 overtime hours per month. For overtime between 45 and 60 hours per month, the law requires companies to "make efforts" to furnish premium pay greater than 25 percent. It mandates premium pay of at least 50 percent for overtime that exceeds 60 hours a month. The law also mandates paid leave on national holidays as well as at least 10 days of paid leave per year following six months of full-time employment. Workers may take five of those 10 days hourly, if agreed by labor and management. The government sets industrial safety and health (ISH) standards.

The Ministry of Health, Labor, and Welfare is responsible for enforcing laws and regulations governing wages, hours, and safety and health standards in most industries. The National Personnel Authority covers government officials. The Ministry of Economy, Trade, and Industry covers ISH standards for mining, and the Ministry of Land, Infrastructure, Transport, and Tourism is responsible for ISH standards in the maritime industry.

The law provides for a fine of up to 500,000 yen ($4,600) for employers who fail to pay a minimum wage, regardless of the number of employees involved or the duration of the violation. Approximately 4,000 labor standards inspectors employed by more than 300 labor standards offices enforced these laws and regulations. Labor unions continued to criticize the government for failing to enforce the law regarding maximum working hours, and workers, including those in government jobs, routinely exceeded the hours outlined in the law.

In general the government effectively enforced applicable ISH law and regulations in all sectors. Penalties for ISH violations included fines and imprisonment. While inspectors have the authority to suspend unsafe operations immediately in cases of flagrant safety violations, in lesser cases they may provide nonbinding shidou (guidance). Workers may remove themselves from situations that endanger health or safety without jeopardy to their employment. Officials within the Ministry of Health, Labor, and Welfare frequently stated that their resources were inadequate to oversee more than 4.3 million firms.

Non-regular workers (which include part-time workers, fixed-term contract workers, and dispatch workers) made up approximately 37 percent of the labor force in 2014. They worked for lower wages and often with less job security and fewer benefits than career workers. Some non-regular workers qualified for various benefits, including insurance, pension, and training. Observers reported a rise in four- or five-year contracts and the termination of contracts shortly before five years--measures that could prevent workers from reaching the five-year point when they may ask their employer to make them permanent employees. Workers in academic positions, such as researchers, technical workers, and teachers in universities, were eligible for 10-year contracts.

Reports of abuses in the TITP were common, including injuries due to unsafe equipment and insufficient training, nonpayment of wages and overtime compensation, excessive and often spurious salary deductions, forced repatriation, and substandard living conditions (also see section 7.b.). In addition, observers noted that a conflict of interest existed, since the inspectors who oversee TITP working conditions were employed by two ministries that are members of the interagency group administering the TITP. Some inspectors appeared reluctant to conduct investigations that could cast a negative light on a government program that business owners favored.

There were also reports of informal employment of foreign asylum seekers on provisional release from detention who did not have work permits. Such workers were vulnerable to mistreatment and did not have access to standard labor protections or oversight.

Falls, road traffic accidents, and injuries caused by heavy machinery were the most common causes of workplace fatalities. The Ministry of Health, Labor, and Welfare also continued to receive applications from family members seeking the ministry's recognition of a deceased individual as a karoshi (death from overwork) victim. In October, in a high profile case, the Tokyo Labor Bureau ruled that a 2015 death of a young woman was a karoshi, after records showed the employee booked 130 hours of overtime in one month and just 10 hours of sleep per week. This finding against a major advertising agency brought renewed attention to the severe consequences of overwork. In October the government released its first white paper on karoshi; it noted that, of 1,700 companies surveyed, 20 percent of them had regular full-time employees who exceeded 80 hours of overtime a month, and 11.9 percent were pushing its workers with overtime exceeding 100 hours. The paper cited 2,159 cases in 2015 of suicides tied to job-related causes, such as exhaustion or bullying. It also reported a record 1,515 compensation claims in fiscal year 2015 for mental disorders caused by work placing a heavy psychological burden on an individual.